Artcoaching Workbook: Created Life System in 12 Easy Monthly Steps

By Nadia Bandura

~~**~~

Copyright 2016 Nadia Bandura

License Notes

* * *

I. Review your life

JANUARY

In the first month, I offer you the following exercises for designing your life:

Everything starts with your thinking.

The way you think determines your emotions. Your emotions determine your actions, and your actions determine your life.

The very first step toward creating the life you want is to become a blank slate. Doing this, you will open doors to new ideas and opportunities.

Think about the best you can bring to your life right now. That would be your strengths and values.

Describe your desired life for the year ahead. The idea is to set your imagination for the year based on your values. This works because when we orient our thinking around our desired images, things tend to fall into place more easily.

 You don't have to know your goals. You just need to imagine your desired life.

FEBRUARY

Coach yourself Exercise 1

Clearing space:

Be present and creatively conscious of what's next. All of this requires clearing out space.

Make a full-on clean sweep through your closets, office, ideas, projects, situations, and ways of being to find what is and what is not evolving with your life right now.

____

____

____

____

____

____

____

____

____

MARCH

If you want happiness, one way is to remove all of the negativity from your life.

Happiness and negativity simply don't co-exist at the same time.

Write down all negative influences in your life.

____

____

____

____

____

____

____

____

____

Coach yourself Exercise 2

Remember you have ultimate control over your own happiness.

You have to remove yourself – as much as possible – from these negative influences.

With some situations, distance is the only way to inoculate you from negativity. It helps if you start building a new circle of friends to avoid your old surroundings.

Try to surround yourself with honest and successful people. Our environment creates our success. Spend more time with people you admire. Try to minimize negative interactions with negative and pessimistic people. Use every moment and every person in order to learn.

APRIL

Coach yourself Exercise 3

Find your inspiration for creating your dream life:

What is always working well in your life?

b. **What is making you happy?**

c. **What are the most important values for you?**

____

____

____

____

____

____

____

____

____

____

d. Identify the values that are being expressed by your heart and write them down

____

____

____

____

____

____

____

____

____

____

II. Design your life

MAY

Happiness and joy of life depend on the harmony of our life areas. Imagine your life as musical scores with all instruments. There are striking parallels between your mind, life system, and an orchestra.

Your mind acts as a conductor and has the task of rehearsing a symphony with all these different groups of instruments.

On your side, you also have to support the first violin, the concertmaster: your creativity.

Creativity consists of a new combination of information. Creativity is the ability to develop new ideas, solutions, and connections. This requires breaking out of the fixed ways of solution structures and learning to think creatively. You have the complete notes of the whole work before you perform your life.

We all have the ability to create the life we want. We just need to learn how to do it. Remember, you only have one life, and it's no dress rehearsal; it's only going to happen once. Take the time right now to work out a design for your life.

Most of the time, the most creative ideas can lead to the most sensible results if you let yourself follow them. Is there an exact "formula"?

There are 3 main areas:

Your professional and social role, your personal happiness, and your independence and ability to enjoy the life you want.

Describe those areas of your life for an exercise.

JUNE

Start creating your life:

1. Pick an aspect of your life that you'd like to improve.

 Don't waste your time and energy blaming and complaining.

Evaluate your experiences and decide if you want to change them or not.

Successful people take full responsibility in order to create the life they want to live.

Create opportunities. You can expect an opportunity in life or try to create it yourself. Focus on what you want, not on how you will achieve this. If you are open to new opportunities — everything becomes possible.

Are you unhappy with some life situations right now? It is your choice to change or leave a situation, and you are responsible for your choices.

2. Once you've imagined the life of your dreams, identify how you want to feel in every specific situation and role in that life:

____

____

____

____

____

____

____

____

____

Stop focusing on what you don't have or don't like.

Focus on what you do have and do like and create a plan for what you think you can create or improve.

Learn your own deepest needs first. Don't be afraid if your choices may disappoint others. That is sometimes necessary in order to grow and live happily.

Those who love you and want the best for you will always accept and support you.

AUGUST

Create your independent life.

3. The next step is simple but important. It takes the time to actually take your responsibility for everything that helps to maintain the main aspects of your life.

Increase your passive income.

Control and minimize your expenses.

Realize your needs and priorities.

Understand that sustained happiness doesn't come from outside circumstances.

You can make your life what you want it to be.

Write down the plan for concrete steps.

III. Live Your Designed Life

SEPTEMBER

"Once we have designed our own life, we must learn how to live it." Nadia Bandura

This is the exercise for living your designed life:

Make concrete plans and keep them flexible enough to be able to change them according to the situation. As the producer of your life, you can change, delete, or add anything you want in your project. But at least by going through this exercise of designing your life, you are in control of your circumstances, rather than allowing yourself to become a victim of them. Do not hesitate to change your path.

OCTOBER

 In accordance with the principle of creativity, all you need to do is follow the easiest way.

Every time when you need to find a solution, ask yourself: how to live in the most efficient manner?

Every time when someone or something is trying to take you out of the way of your created life, do not rush to resist. Calm yourself and watch what happens.

Every time you need something to be done, ask yourself: which way is the easiest?

NOVEMBER

Go with the flow.

Activate inside creativity. First feel it and then act.

Let your life go with the flow and see how you feel better.

Some people just get what happens. You will create all the things you want and intend to have.

DECEMBER

Turn yourself into the creator of your destiny.

In fact, what can be learned from this?

Our mind cannot always guarantee a solution. Now imagine that you do not resist the flow, but not randomly drifting like a paper boat. Move in harmony with the present, noticing dangerous areas that appear, and keeping the chosen direction. The wheel is in your hands. Of course, first, you must choose the correct general direction. The direction is determined by the chosen goal and the way to achieve it. Once a direction is chosen, it should be possible to avoid sudden unwanted movements.

And, whenever it is possible, consider life as an art.

A powerful intellect of the mind cannot decide anything if the solution already exists in the space of creativity. If you do not climb into the jungle of solutions and do not interfere with the flow of options, the decision will come by itself. For example, the creative process is based on several unproven postulates, because, in some cases, the object of the creation is a result of artist's imagination. Be in harmony with nature.

Nature does not waste energy. In other words, our mind is looking for sophisticated solutions to simple problems. People do not have time to explain this nature. Scientists are attempting to unite the various manifestations of reality, but it is hardly possible. Multiphase of our world is the world's first fundamental quality.

All these arguments may seem too abstract. But you can practically see the existence of the power of creativity. This is truly a magnificent gift of life. In every issue, there are within it the encrypted keys to its solution. The first key - move along the path of least resistance. People tend to look for complex solutions. Creating already contains the solutions to all problems. And most of the problems are artificially created for the same reason.

And my last word – whatever you do, leave space for creativity and miracles in the year ahead.

Have a great year!